WHO IS SANTA CLAUS?

WHO IS SANTA CLAUS?
The true story behind a living legend.

ROBIN CRICHTON

illustrated by

MARGARET NISBET

CANONGATE

First published 1987
by Canongate Publishing Limited
17 Jeffrey Street, Edinburgh

British Library Cataloguing in Publication Data
Crichton, Robin
Who is Santa Claus?:the truth behind a living legend.
I. Nicholas, *Saint* II. Santa Claus
III. Christian Saints—Turkey—Lysia—Biography
I. Title II. Margaret Nisbet
398'.352 GT4992
ISBN 0-86241-160-2

The television series 'The Curious Case of Santa Claus' was
produced for Channel 4 by Edinburgh Film Productions.

Typeset by Alan Sutton Publishing Limited, Gloucester, England
Printed by The Bath Press, Bath, England

to Margaret, Sian, and Louise
who first asked the question,
and to Trish who set me looking for the answer.

CONTENTS

ACKNOWLEDGEMENTS

I would like to record a very special indebtedness to the following people and organisations without whose specialist knowledge and assistance much of this book would not have been possible.

Padres Gerardo Cioffari and Damiano Bova, whose dedicated and detailed research on the life of Saint Nicholas has made them perhaps the greatest living authorities on the subject; the Waterleigh Bottom Players, whose enthusiasm helped to keep alive the disappearing tradition of mumming in England; Celal Hafifbilek and Erkut Tackin in Turkey; Gerry van der Molen and Gerard de Klerk in the Netherlands; Margrit Jackson in Sweden; André Ruesch in Switzerland; Andras Peterffy in Hungary; and in the USA Mary Ann Long, the postmistress of Santa Claus, Indiana; Jenny Zink of Western Temporary Services; Detective Kleinlein of the New York Police Department; Richard Martin of North Pole, New York; Professor Anne Marie Salgat of the General Theological Seminary in New York; the Public Relations Department of Macy's; and not least Bob Larbey who wrote the screenplay for *The Curious Case of Santa Claus* and Naomi Sargant who commissioned it for Channel Four.

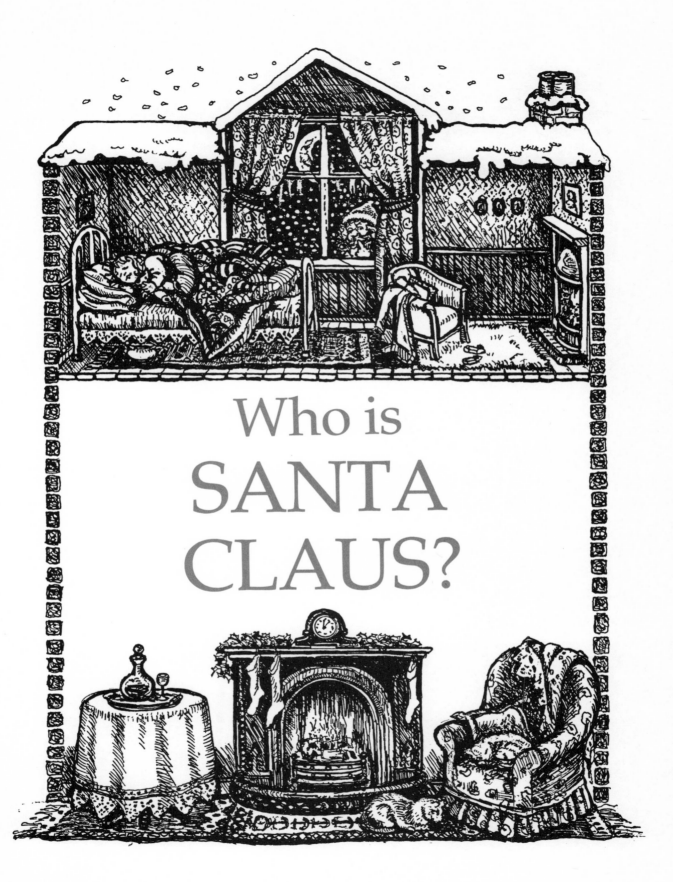

Who is
SANTA
CLAUS?

Can you remember being three or four years old and seeing Santa Claus for the first time? Did he come in the middle of the night as a shrouded stranger prowling in the shadows of your darkened room? Or was he that God-like figure, robed in red, on a tinsel throne in a department store?

Either way, a first encounter with Santa Claus can be a pretty disturbing experience. He is gigantic in those extraordinary padded clothes and looks as if he has not had a haircut in a hundred years. In fact he is not at all dissimilar to the down-and-outs you sometimes see lying on public benches – the sort Mummy always told you never to talk to!

'Ho! Ho! Ho!' he bellows. No-one ever said *that* to you before. Then before you know it, you have been hoisted on to his knee and he is smothering you in *bonhomie* and bad breath! And you cannot really be blamed if you become hysterical because you get it mixed up with 'Fee! Fie! Fo! Fum!' and visions of a child-eating ogre.

Then there is the story of the Three Wise Men and how they followed a star to find a baby in a manger.

Where does Santa Claus fit into all that? Did he follow the star too and come down the chimney? Don't burglars come down the chimney? It is all very confusing!

When I was growing up in Scotland during the 1940s, Christmas was not a holiday. If you took the train north from England, as soon as you crossed the Border, the lights on the Christmas trees would vanish in a Calvinist darkness. Christmas Day in Scotland was just an ordinary working day. It had been made a Bank Holiday in 1871, but apart from bankers, everyone else just went to work as usual. The post was delivered in the morning. Daily newspapers were on the newstands, shops and offices were open for business, and no-one grieved for the lack of a holiday they had never known.

The Scottish mid-winter festival was, and still is, Hogmanay; a Bacchanalian adventure, with no religious overtones, which starts on New Year's Eve and goes on for as many days as stamina permits.

In the fifties television arrived, bringing with it a special season of Christmas programming. Gradually fewer people went to work on Christmas Day and Santa Claus began to appear in the more exclusive department stores. In the sixties Britain joined the European Economic Community and Christmas was expanded to an official two-day holiday.

I myself always ignored Christmas. But then I got married. My wife is half Welsh, half English. As our first Christmas approached, she suggested we should buy some decorations for the house, and perhaps have a Christmas tree. It had never occurred to me that a woman of such normally impeccable taste would want to festoon our house with glittering tat! However, being greatly in love, I compromised, but only on the strict understanding that we would not spend any money on decorations; we would make them. The results were dreadful – paper

chains made from old newspapers, and mobiles from wire coat-hangers. They went up and quickly came down again leaving us with a few stars made out of straw, and ivy from the garden wall. The next year I admitted defeat and we went shopping.

So it was that as an adult I began to discover Christmas. Three daughters were born in the space of two years, and all the magic of stockings and presents had to be introduced. Inevitably, one day the question came; 'Daddy, who is Santa Claus?'

Some time before, while I was making a film in Turkey, I had discovered that St Nicholas had been born there. The combination of my daughter's question and this titbit of knowledge sparked off the idea for another film – a quest to discover the truth about Santa Claus.

I discovered that he is simply the youngest of a quite remarkable and highly international family. His relatives are scattered all over the world – there is Sinter Klaas in the Netherlands, Father Christmas in England, the Weihnachtsmann in Germany, San Nicola in Italy, the Jultomten and Julnisse in Scandinavia, and Nikolai Chudovorits in Russia, to name but a few. But they have one thing in common – they are all connected with a man called Nicholas who was born seventeen hundred years ago in what is now south-west Turkey.

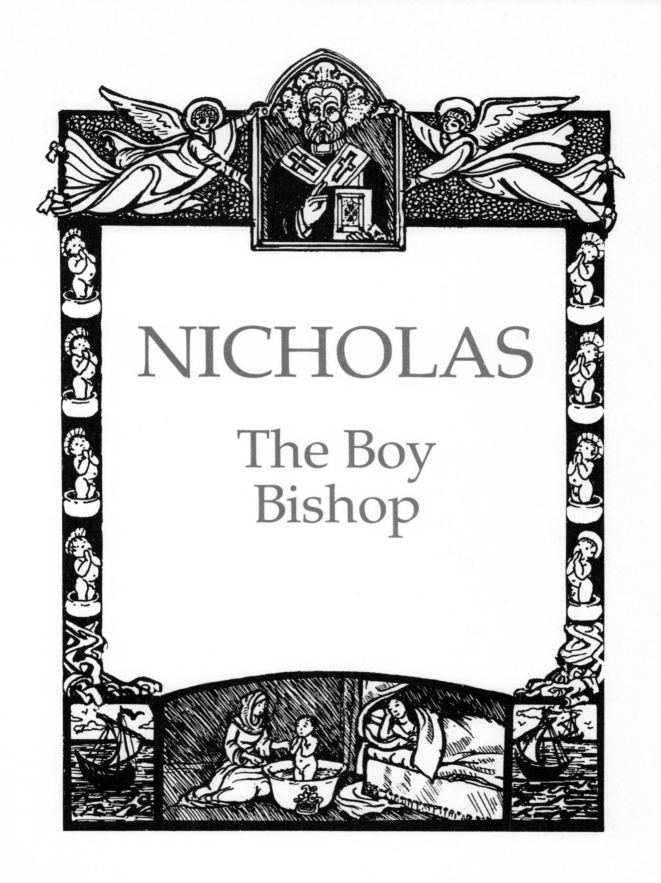

NICHOLAS

The Boy Bishop

The coast of south-west Turkey is one of the most beautiful places in the world. The Taurus Mountains drop from 10,000 feet almost sheer into the sea – scenically stunning but a graveyard for ships, with only the occasional harbour where a mountain river has built up a small coastal plain. In the seventh century BC, Greek colonists settled here. Gradually a chain of cities developed, each isolated from its neighbours by wild mountain ranges but linked by the regular sea routes between the Near East and Europe. The province was known as Lycia. It lasted for nearly two thousand years, until at the end of the 14th century it fell to the Turks.

The Turks, traditionally nomadic herdsmen from the steppes of Asia, had no interest in cities. They were farmers – country people with their roots in the land. A few of the old Greek cities were resettled but most were simply abandoned. The streets were left to grass over. There was no need to destroy the buildings or even to steal their stones. Only now are they being rediscovered and recognised as some of the most impressive monuments of the classical world.

But what the Turks left alone, nature has altered. The Taurus mountains lie along a major fault in the Earth's crust and are prone to earthquakes. The city of Simena, for

example, was turned into an Atlantis: the ruins of the northern part remain part of the mainland, but what is left of the southern side is now on an island; the area between them lies at the bottom of the sea. If you look down through the clear blue water you can see the remains of streets and houses with barnacle-encrusted pots still lying where the earthquake left them.

Patara, built at the mouth of the Xanthos, was a major Lycian city and, in its day, one of the busiest ports of the classical world. As the result of an earthquake the river changed course, the harbour silted up, and sand dunes cut it off from the sea. The lighthouse, which once marked the headland, today sits on a hill 600 metres from the shore. It is a classical ghost town. A triumphal arch rises surrealistically out of a wheatfield. An amphitheatre lies half buried in the sand. Great ramparts still shelter the remains of shops and houses. Bathhouses endure as monuments to the wealthy merchants who built them, and on the Western Quay the granaries, established by the Emperor Hadrian, still stand at roof height.

The Roman Empire

At the beginning of the second century AD, after Lycia had become a province of the Roman Empire, Patara was at the height of its prosperity. It was known not only for its port but also as a major centre of divination and astrology. Perhaps it was the fame of Patara's Temple of Apollo which took St Paul there on one of his missionary journeys. He left behind him a small group of Christian converts, which gradually grew. They built a church and became an established and influential minority in the town. For the most part they were middle class people – merchants, craftsmen, and small landowners.

According to an anonymously written manuscript, now housed in the Coptic Museum in Cairo, this Christian community included a couple called Epiphaneos and Nona who lived in the western part of the city, not far from the sea. Although they had been married for thirty years, they had never managed to have a family and had given up hope of ever having children. So, when, after all those years of hope and prayer, Nona became pregnant, it seemed like a miracle.

The baby was a boy. It is recorded that immediately after his birth, he stood up in his bath and raised his arms as if praying to God. Even more remarkable, apparently, was his consistent refusal to suckle his mother until after sundown on Wednesdays and Fridays, the fast days of the early Christians.

His parents christened him Nicholas, after an uncle who was Father Superior of a monastery at Xanthos, a city

seven miles up river from Patara. Their great ambition was that the boy would follow in his uncle's footsteps and go into the Church, and, to this end, they set out to give him the best education possible. But when he was in his teens an epidemic swept through Lycia, decimating the population. Both Epiphaneos and Nona died, leaving Nicholas orphaned and alone. His uncle arranged for him to enter the monastery at Xanthos, but first, Nicholas had to give away all his worldly goods.

Legend holds that a neighbouring family had fallen on hard times. The father had once been a wealthy man, but a combination of bad luck and bad judgement had lost him everything. His three daughters were all of an age to marry, but their chances were slim because their father could no longer afford to provide them with dowries. And without a dowry a girl could not wed. The girls had talked the problem over amongst themselves and concluded that the only practical solution would be for the eldest sister to go into a brothel *to abandon [herself] to the synne of lecherye so that by the gayne and wynning of [her] infamye [the others might] be sustained.*

Rumours soon spread round the neighbourhood and eventually reached Nicholas. He waited until the early hours of the morning when the whole town was asleep. Putting some gold coins in a small bag, he disguised himself in a hooded cloak, and slipped out into the street.

The following morning the girls awoke and, when one of them reached out for her clothes as usual, she found the little bag of gold. Some say it was lying in a shoe, others that it was in a stocking.

The next night a second bag of gold arrived anonymously through the window. 'Who could their mysterious benefactor be?', they wondered. Their father was determined to find out. On the third night he stayed awake and, as soon as he heard the tell-tale thud, rushed out of the house just in time to glimpse the cloaked figure turning the corner. He gave chase. With no chance of getting away, Nicholas turned to face him. He was highly embarrassed and made the father swear never to reveal his identity. The father must eventually have told someone, for the story survived and in time became the basis of the almost universal tradition of hanging up a stocking or putting out a shoe to be miraculously filled with gifts during the night.

Nicholas studied for the priesthood under the tutelage of his uncle, eventually persuading him to send him on a pilgrimage to the Holy Land. In the three hundred years since the drama of Christ's agony and crucifixion, the Romans had completely destroyed the Jerusalem that He knew. The city was a focus for religious confrontation. Jewish temples had been replaced by Roman ones and many of the sites associated with Jesus's last days were buried beneath the buildings of a new Roman city. But the small Christian community which gave shelter to Nicholas

still knew their location and were the hub of a faith which was spreading throughout the Empire.

After a stay of several months, the time came for Nicholas to return. The voyage out had been calm and uneventful, but the journey back was just the opposite. The weather started fair, but when they were about half way home a gale struck, and for two days and two nights the little vessel tried to ride out the storm. As the waves crashed over the bows, Nicholas prayed for their deliverance and the sailors prayed with him.

At dawn on the third day they sighted land and found themselves off Myra, the capital of Lycia — only about twenty miles east of Patara. As they limped into harbour, Nicholas's first thought was to find a church where he

could give thanks to God for their survival. But, unbeknown to him, a convocation was taking place in Myra. The old Bishop of Myra had decided to retire, and all the bishops of Lycia had come together to appoint his successor. They had been praying for guidance and the previous night one of them had reported a vision. An angel had appeared and told him to gather together all the other bishops before first light to wait inside the main door of the church. *Whomsoever shall be first to enter shall be worthy of the office. His name is Nicholas.* So it was that when Nicholas arrived at the church, he found the bishops awaiting him. They asked his name and, though he was still in his teens, he was immediately acclaimed as the new Bishop of Myra.

Throughout the Roman Empire Christians had been tolerated as a religious minority. But in 303, the Emperor Diocletian ordered their persecution and a return to the worship of the old gods. Nicholas was imprisoned, together with all those in his congregation who refused to renounce their faith. Yet in his cell he received visitors and sent out letters, keeping his flock secretly together and their faith alive.

Two years later Diocletian abdicated, and the army on the Rhine proclaimed Constantine as the new Emperor. But he was not unopposed, and it was only after six years of gradually strengthening his position that Constantine was ready to march on Rome. In the late summer of 312 AD he crossed the Alps and prepared to lay siege to the seat of the Roman Empire.

Although he had never enforced Diocletian's edict of persecution, Constantine was not a Christian. He was in fact a strong follower of the Sun God. Years later, the Bishop of Caesarea recorded Constantine's own account of an experience which shaped the history of the world:

> *He called to God with earnest prayer and supplication that He would reveal to him who He was and stretch forth His right hand to help him in his present dangers. And while he was thus praying, a most marvellous sign appeared to him from heaven. He said that about noon he saw with his own eyes, a cross of light in the heavens above the sun, and bearing the inscription:*

> BY THIS SIGN THOU SHALT CONQUER.

> *At this divine sign he was struck by amazement as was his whole army, which also witnessed the miracle.*

The most plausible explanation is that they witnessed a solar halo which can sometimes appear cruciform. Whatever it was, Constantine believed that the Christian God had revealed Himself and promised him victory. The night before the battle for Rome, Constantine dreamed that he was ordered to mark his soldiers shields with the sign of the cross. This he duly did. His subsequent victory made him Emperor of Rome. It also convinced him that the Christian God was the true God and that he, Constantine, was His chosen vessel.

Thus Constantine became the first Christian Emperor of Rome. One of his first decrees was to order the release of all Christians. In his diocese, Nicholas set about the destruction, once and for all, of the pagan temples. Perhaps he was also behind the destruction of the famous Temple of Apollo at Patara, of which, without excavation, no visible traces remain.

Christianity, previously a minority religion, was suddenly endowed with political importance. Twelve years after Constantine became Emperor of the Western Empire, he invaded and took the Eastern Empire. Once again the Christian God gave him His protection and support, and by command of God he gave his name to a new Rome, a second capital of the Empire – Constantinople, the first wholly Christian city in the world. Thus in 324 AD the Roman Empire was for the last time reunited under one Emperor.

For years Christianity had existed in a series of isolated pockets, and as the mantle of persecution was lifted it revealed a bewildering number of conflicting views on doctrine and more importantly on the nature of Christ. In 325 AD Constantine decreed that the Christian Church should agree a common creed. All the bishops were summoned to Nicaea in the north of Asia Minor for what was to be the first general council of the Christian Church.

For Nicholas, it meant a long journey. That summer there had been a terrible drought and everywhere there

was famine. People were starving. The crops had failed and all the livestock had been eaten. Nicholas arrived at a small village where he hoped to find shelter at the inn but really did not expect any food. The innkeeper was overwhelmed by the honour of receiving such an important guest. Intent on making a good impression, he offered Nicholas a pot roast for supper. Nicholas was delighted after so many days of hunger, but gradually his surprise turned to suspicion. Where in this lifeless landscape could there still be an animal to be eaten? He made his way to the kitchen, and there he found the innkeeper preparing to chop up three little boys who had been killed and pickled in brine. Horrified, Nicholas fell to his knees in prayer. The impossible happened, and before the innkeeper's astonished gaze, the three boys came back to life. The innkeeper was instantly converted to Christianity. But what was to be done with the three boys? Nicholas founded an orphanage. The story spread and, in time, Nicholas became known as the patron saint of children.

At Nicaea the debate was long and often heated – so heated, in fact, that at one point, it is said, Nicholas lost his temper and punched a fellow bishop on the nose! He

returned to Myra in due course, and went on to perform many more miracles – all faithfully chronicled by his biographers. Their original accounts no longer exist but they were copied over and over again in the centuries which followed.

One miracle is particularly important to his fame as a gift-giver, and once again it occurred after a bad harvest. The granaries were only half full, and everyone feared a winter of famine. During the autumn a fleet of merchantmen came into harbour at Myra, seeking shelter from a storm. They were carrying grain from Constantinople to Alexandria. Nicholas convinced other ships' captains that if they gave the Lycians enough grain to survive the winter, their holds would nevertheless be full by the time they reached Alexandria. He was very persuasive. The merchants unloaded their ships and, sure enough, by the time they arrived at Alexandria, they found Nicholas's promise had come true. Nicholas had saved his people with another miracle, and the sailors carried his reputation to all corners of the Mediterranean.

In time the fresh-faced boy bishop grew into a white-haired old man with a patriarchal beard. He died on 6th December 342 AD and was buried in a richly carved tomb in the church where he had spent so much of his life. Buried, but not forgotten, for he continued to work his miracles, and his tomb became a shrine. From the tomb came a mysterious liquid endowed with remarkable properties of healing. They called it the Manna of St Nicholas and the sick came from far and wide to be cured of their ailments. Only the smallest drop would provide the most remarkable results.

His fame increased, and he became venerated as a saint. His biography was translated into every Christian language – Greek, Latin, Armenian, Syrian, Slav, and even Arabic. The Church at Myra became known at the Church of St Nicholas and 6th December as his feast day.

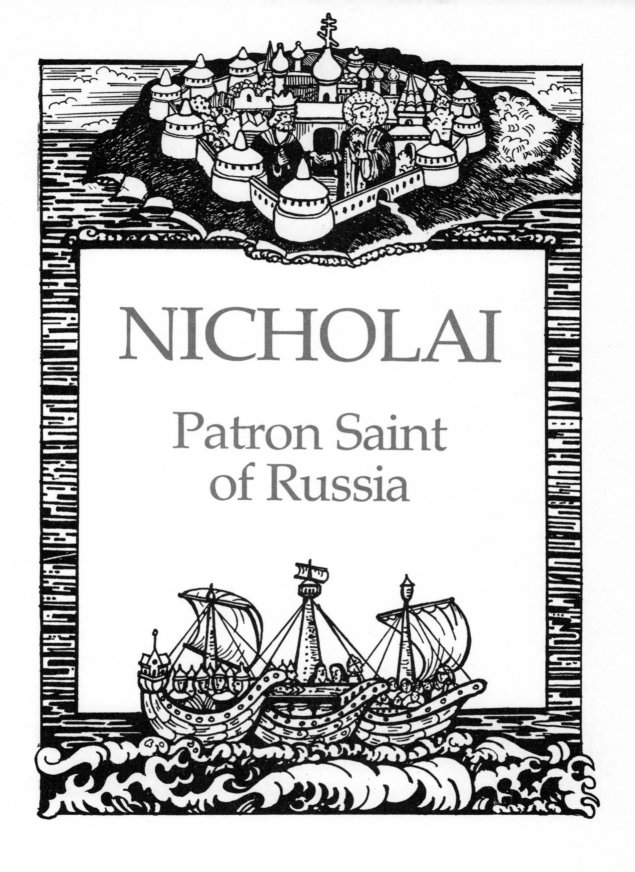

NICHOLAI

Patron Saint
of Russia

rom the eighth century onwards a human whirlwind from Scandinavia blew across the known world and beyond. Over a period of three hundred years, Scandinavian long ships sailed north and west, colonising Iceland and Ireland, discovering Greenland and America. In the East they penetrated inland down the Dnieper to Byzantium and down the Volga to the Arabian world. These men of the north – Nor'men – had a great talent for organisation. Wherever they settled in Europe they streamlined the feudal system, sub-dividing their lands into knights' fiefs and controlling them through census accounts like the Domesday Book.

Along the two great rivers Dnieper and Volga they established forts to protect their traders from the dangers of marauding Slavs. Gradually the Nor'men united the various tribes and established themselves as a ruling class, laying the foundations of a state which would one day become Russia but for the moment was a principality with its capital at Kiev. For over a hundred years the Nor'men of Kiev harassed the frontiers of Byzantium, but in 944 a trade treaty at last brought peace and opened the princi-

pality to Christian influence.

The Patriarch of Constantinople was convinced that the best way to secure his frontier would be to convert Kiev to Christianity. St Cyril and St Methodius were commissioned to translate the scriptures into Slav, and armed with the Word, missionaries quickly began to win converts. As the new faith gained a foothold, so relations between Kiev and Constantinople steadily improved. In 987 a marriage was arranged between the Byzantine Emperor's sister and the Grand Duke of Kiev. As his public conversion would establish Christianity as the religion of all the people, the Church diplomatically overlooked the existence of his four other wives and innumerable concubines!

With Christianity came magnificent Byzantine icons and wonderful tales of St Nicholas. In Kiev, work started on a cathedral dedicated to St Nicholas, and the Saint's reputation for miracles grew almost daily.

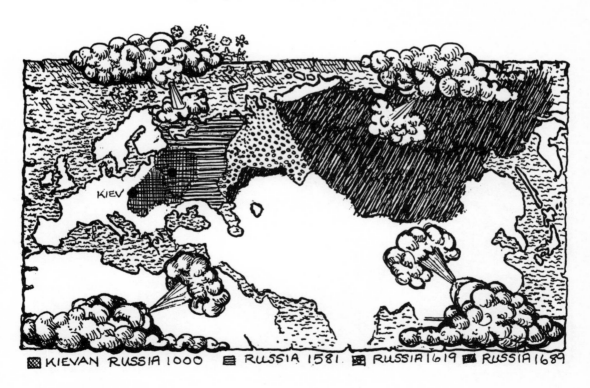

KIEV

⊞ KIEVAN RUSSIA 1000　▤ RUSSIA 1581.　▨ RUSSIA 1619　▨ RUSSIA 1689

One Sunday, a young couple were walking home from church with their baby. Crossing the bridge over the Dnieper the child slipped from his mother's arms and was lost in the foaming waters of the river. The parents were utterly distraught and prayed to St Nicholas that by some miracle their child might be saved. The following morning, when the sacristan went to open up the cathedral, he was astonished to hear a baby crying. There beneath the icon of St Nicholas lay the infant – soaking wet, but alive and well.

St Nicholas became known as Nikolai Chudovorits – the Wonder Worker. The tales of his miracles captured the imagination of the Russian people, and even to this day the Christians of Russia address their prayers to both Christ and St Nicholas.

In the centuries which followed, the centre of power moved from Kiev to Moscow and the Russian principalities became united under a tsar. The new Russian

empire gradually expanded eastwards. Waves of missionaries spread through the untamed regions beyond the Urals, taking their patron St Nicholas with them.

By the seventeenth century they had reached Siberia, and it was here that Nikolai, the Wonder Worker, came into contact with the reindeer people – the tribes of nomadic herdsmen living to the north of the Arctic Circle. Reindeer were the measure of a man's wealth: they provided clothing, food and transport; to survive, a family needed about a thousand head.

In the summer the people lived in tents, moving with their herds along the seasonal pastures of the coast and river valleys. In winter they migrated to the milder weather inland where, during the months of darkness, they lived in timber huts, the roofs supported by a large central pole. These dwellings had no real chimney as we know it, just a hole to let the smoke out. In winter the huts became buried under the snow, and the only way in or out was by a ladder through the smoke-hole.

To live in the Arctic is to live on the limits of human endurance. Two hundred years ago it was even harsher than it is today, and magic and religion were very important elements in survival. In the mythology of the reindeer people, the world was represented as a tree. Its roots were in the land of the dead, the underworld; its top reached the heavens, the realm of the guardian spirits. The central pole symbolised the world-tree. Notches carved into it represented different levels of heaven.

Communication between the world of men and the world of spirits was effected through a medium of Shaman: part priest, part medicine man, and part mystic. In his role as priest he served as the intermediary between

the land of the living and the underworld of the dead. He escorted the deceased on their final journey from this world to join their ancestors. On occasions he could arrange a return trip. A promise of suitable offerings might persuade a ghost to come back and dwell for a year or two in the living world as guardian of the reindeer. In their timber huts, smoke from the fire carried the peoples' prayers to the heavens. The Shamans brought the response. They were the messengers of the Gods.

As a medicine man the Shaman dealt not just with physical ills, but with spiritual ones as well. Above all, he was a mystic and a master of divination. It was believed that every man had two souls. One was his physical soul, which was confined to his body; the other was his spirit, which could move out of the body and travel independently through space and time.

If a man fell ill, there could only be two possible reasons. Either a malignant spirit had entered the body, in which case the Shaman would use ritual and magic, combined with any natural remedies he might have, to extract it. Or else the ailing man's own spirit had travelled out of his body on a trip and had either got lost or been stolen by evil spirits. To retrieve it, the Shaman would have to travel out of his body and journey to the other world. This enabled him to visit and report on distant places and people, as a sort of primitive time-traveller. The visions he experienced on these trips were the source of his specialised knowledge for dealing with ills, both in the present and in the future.

In midwinter the ceremony of Annual Renewal took place. The Shaman would induce a trance and at a certain

stage in the proceedings start to climb the pole, using the notches as steps, on a symbolic journey to the other worlds before finally disappearing through the smoke-hole in the roof of the hut. To assist him on his supernatural journeys, he was accompanied by various animal spirits. A bird guided him to the upper world; he rode a fish to the underworld. To protect him he had a supernatural reindeer, his bodyguard, which would fight off

attacks by other supernatural reindeer belonging to any rival Shaman who might wish him ill.

To induce the necessary state of mind, the Shaman depended on hallucinogenic plants and magic mushrooms. Fly Agaric was particularly good. It created a sense of weightlessness, of floating in space. Fly Agaric is the fairy toadstool of children's picture books – bright red with white spots – which grows wherever there are birch trees. In the Arctic it was highly prized and a man would barter a whole reindeer or two to obtain a single mushroom. Usually it was kept in a dried form. The mushroom could then either be eaten or alternatively boiled in water to produce a liquid to which berry juice might be added to disguise the unpleasant flavour. Frowned on by the civilising forces of the west, the use of Fly Agaric has been in retreat for over 400 years. It is still used occasionally to help round up reindeer, but for human consumption it has been supplanted by Vodka and other forms of 'fire water'. The stimulant may have changed but the psychological need to escape from the harsh day-to-day struggle

for survival is as strong as ever.

From the earliest days of Christianity, the policy of missionaries had always been to adapt and incorporate pagan customs by giving them a Christian interpretation and meaning. And the Arctic was no exception, Nikolai became a Super Shaman, a spiritual time-traveller, a mystic go-between for the people and their new Christian God. On his visits to the reindeer people, like the Shaman – and indeed everyone else – he came and went through the chimney – literally – in a cloud of smoke!

Shamanism, once common to all the Arctic peoples is nowadays officially dead. The peoples of the Arctic are still mainly herdsmen, and reindeer still the basis of the economy, but hardship is lessened by social welfare, and people are more likely to travel by snow-scooter than reindeer sleigh!

Nikolai Chudovorits is now little more than a folk memory. But in the dark midwinter of 200 years ago he was flying high on magic mushrooms, carrying gifts for the Gods on his supernatural reindeer sledge and returning to the mortal world down the chimney.

The Norman Empire

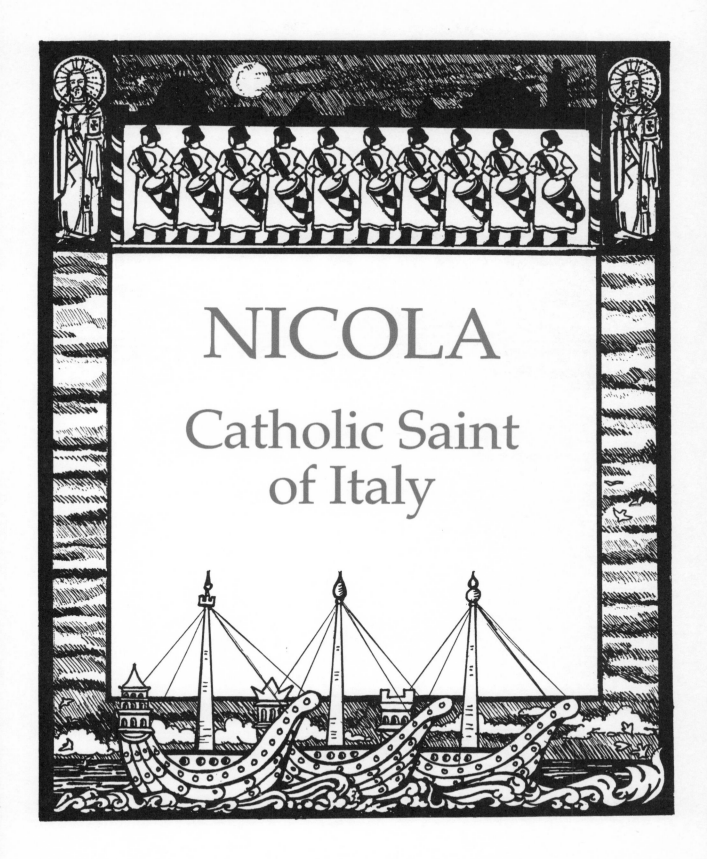

NICOLA

Catholic Saint
of Italy

By the end of the 10th century Christianity had brought peace to Byzantium's northern frontier with the conversion of Kiev, but the rest of the Empire was disintegrating. In the East, in 1071, the Turks annihilated the Byzantine army, leaving the farmlands of the interior open to roving bands of Tartar horsemen. In the Mediterranean a decline in sea power had left the rich coastal cities unprotected against the raids of pirates. In Southern Italy the last of the Byzantine strongholds had fallen to the Normans, who were now about to capture Sicily from the Arabs, and launch an attack on Greece and Thrace. Through the First Crusade they would acquire Antioch, in what is now

Syria, and make it a Norman Principality. They looked set to become the new masters of Byzantium itself.

The Nor'men who had settled in Europe had developed into a great new force. In the 10th century they had become the Dukes of Normandy, and in the 11th they had conquered England, where their Duke became a King. And where they did not go as conquerors they went as mercenaries and traders. While half the armies of Europe were led by Norman soldiers, Norman sailors dominated the trade routes, maintaining links with the homelands but travelling to the extremities of the civilised world.

Norman ships called at Myra and their crews came to hear of the reputation of St Nicholas. Wherever they sailed they heard innumerable stories of how, against impossible odds, he had miraculously saved men from drowning and shipwreck. Ever since the miracle with the grain ships, St Nicholas had been an increasingly important protector of sailors. What he could do for others, he could do for the Normans. Like so much else that they had made their own, the Normans accepted St Nicholas as a powerful patron.

In the Spring of 1087, three Norman ships bringing grain from their kingdom in Southern Italy arrived in Antioch. The port was buzzing with the news of a recent attack on Myra by pirates. The coast was no longer safe and it was rumoured that a Venetian expedition planned to remove St Nicholas's remains from Myra and take them to safety in Venice.

The Norman sailors decided to beat the Venetians to it.

They immediately set sail and arrived at Myra, posing as pilgrims. It was not until they had gathered round St Nicholas's tomb that they revealed their true purpose. The monks were horrified to learn that their intention was to desecrate the shrine and take the Saint's remains to Italy! They threatened to rouse the town if the sailors did not leave peaceably. But the sailors were not to be deterred. Tempers flared; belligerence was met with counter threats. One of the brothers grabbed the vial of Manna which was kept on the tomb. It slipped and crashed on the stone floor. Miraculously it did not break. Was this a sign from St Nicholas?

Three of the monks recalled a vision they had received after Myra had been raided by pirates the year before. St Nicholas had appeared to tell them that if the people who had fled to the mountains did not return to Myra, he would leave. Many had in fact never come back and now the monks realised that perhaps the prophecy was about to be fulfilled.

The Normans promised to build St Nicholas a magnificent basilica in Bari, the capital of their new Italian kingdom. While the monks reluctantly looked on, the sailors broke open the tomb. A brother gathered up the Saint's remains in his cloak and agreed to accompany

them on the journey. Word of what had happened soon spread through the town. People flocked to the harbour to plead with the Normans. Without St Nicholas to protect them their city was surely doomed. They waded into the water, accusing the monks of treachery and trying to grasp the ships' oars to prevent them from leaving.

By the time the ships finally got away, the sun was setting. With the wind set fair they made Patara in two days, but then the weather changed. Every time they put to sea, they were blown back to port. It seemed that St Nicholas did not want to go to Italy after all. Why the change of heart? It came to light that some of the sailors had taken the odd bone as a personal talisman. Once his remains were gathered together again and placed in a casket, the wind veered round and the little fleet finally set out for Italy.

Three weeks later, on 9th May, they arrived at Bari. The whole town was gathered on the quayside to give them a triumphal welcome. The sailors told the crowd of their promise to build a magnificent new basilica, but some people took the view that it would be more appropriate for him to be placed in the cathedral. The archbishop was away, and the senior prelate, the abbot of the Benedictine

monastery, suggested that to allow time for debate the remains should temporarily lie in the abbey.

At least two mediaeval chroniclers record that San Nicola, as he was called in Italian, immediately embarked on a spate of miracles. In the first twenty-four hours, he healed no fewer than forty-seven incurable cases. On the second day, he managed another twenty-two, and the day after that, a further twenty-nine. Pilgrims started arriving in droves.

When the Archbishop returned, he made straight for the abbey, announcing his intention of transporting the Saint's remains to the Cathedral immediately. A deputation of townspeople tried to reason with him but when it became obvious he was going to resort to force, the confrontation escalated into a riot and three people were killed. The townspeople regained possession of the relics and finally the whole matter was resolved when the Pope himself intervened and placed San Nicola under the direct jurisdiction of the Holy See.

A fine Norman basilica was erected on the site of the old Byzantine governor's palace. Today it claims to be the only shrine in the Christian world shared jointly by the Roman Catholic and Orthodox Churches. In the Basilica, beside San Nicola's tomb, is a small Orthodox chapel. It was consecrated in 1966 and is the first place, since the schism of the Roman Catholic and Orthodox Churches in 1054, that the Orthodox Liturgy has been allowed within the walls of a Roman Catholic church.

Every May Bari celebrates the great events of 1087 in an annual festival. On 8th May pilgrims begin to gather. At

the doorway of the Basilica they sink to their knees and shuffle slowly and painfully forward up the flagstones of the nave. At San Nicola's altar emotion often becomes ecstasy. Some are in tears; some faint; others appear possessed and speak in tongues. As one group moves away from the altar, the next are already on their knees at the main door. During the course of the day hundreds, if not thousands, of worshippers pass through the church.

In the evening the old Norman castle is floodlit. Rank upon rank of mediaeval drummers and heralds troop through the main gate in a torchlight parade. The procession through the town is over a mile long. At the rear, a replica of a mediaeval sailing ship is hauled by sixty-two men, the number of the sailors and merchants who were on the original expedition of 1087.

The pageant is the prelude to the main religious festival which always takes place on 9th May, the day San Nicola arrived in Bari. It starts with a mass in the Basilica. Then, at six in the morning, a life-size statue of San Nicola appears in the square – carried shoulder high by a party of pall-bearers. The town band strikes up a rollicking Italian tune. The pall-bearers move to the beat of the music with a curious rocking shuffle and San Nicola sways off into the narrow streets of the town. It seems as if the whole of Bari is out to greet him. Every doorway, every window, every alleyway is crowded with families watching him pass. At the quayside, the Archbishop pours Manna on the waters and blesses the sea. For the rest of the day San Nicola floats on a platform in the middle of the harbour, while boats of every size carry pilgrims back and forth. Only

after the sun has set does he return ashore.

The following day one final ceremony takes place. When the Normans brought San Nicola's bones to Bari they brought with them the miracle of the Manna. This remarkable liquid, which first made St Nicholas famous in Myra 1600 years ago, is now extracted from the tomb in Bari once a year. It is the climax to the whole religious festival. On the morning of 10th May the Father Prior crawls into the Saint's tomb. With a narrow pipette he extracts the Manna which has collected there. Analysis has revealed it to be a very pure form of water. It contains none of the distinctive elements of the local supply, and so far there has been no satisfactory scientific explanation of how it is formed or where it comes from. The Manna is diluted with ordinary water and sold to pilgrims and townsfolk, who preserve it for times of sickness. Many local families have their own traditional Manna bottles, often hundreds of years old, painted with colourful religious scenes.

In the crypt of the Basilica, there hangs a magnificent Byzantine icon of St Nicholas. It was donated by the Tsar of Serbia, Stephen Uros III (1281–1321) who is depicted in the bottom corners with his first queen, Helen. Uros divorced Helen, and two further wives, and married Simonida, the Byzantine Empress's daughter. She was five years old and he was forty-five. Although he had vowed to wait ten years before consumating the marriage, he broke his promise after only two or three. The psy-

chological damage was perhaps greater than the physical. Unable ever to bear children, Simonida grew up into an embittered and malevolent woman.

Uros already had a son and heir by Helen, Stephen, who was actually older than Simonida. When she was nineteen, Simonida informed the King of a plot by her stepson to take the throne and his father's life. Simonida's accusation was totally unfounded, but nevertheless Uros had his son bound and blinded. For greater security Simonida then persuaded Uros to send Stephen with his two children to be imprisoned in Constantinople. He was incarcerated in a monastery where his exemplary behaviour won the admiration of the monks and even the Emperor, who began to visit him quite regularly and seek his advice on how to deal with religious disputes.

After five years in jail, on 6th November Stephen had a vision. St Nicholas appeared to him promising to restore his sight. Sure enough when he removed the bandages from his eyes, he found he could see once more, but, frightened of what his stepmother might engineer, he kept it a secret. By now Uros had become aware of his wife's psychosis. He had only himself to blame. By making him punish his son she had made him punish himself. Everything he heard of his son was good and he was full of remorse. Eventually he asked the Emperor to allow him to come home. Stephen forgave his father, and the icon dates from the time of their reunion.

From the Norman basilica in Bari Nicholas found his

way all over Europe.

During the tenth and eleventh centuries the Normans dominated Europe, and wherever they went, St Nicholas went with them. He made his way up the great trading rivers – the Meuse and Moselle, the Rhine and the Rhone, the Danube, the Dnieper and the Don. He was already the patron saint of sailors and children. Now along these rivers, he became the patron of towns and trading posts. And within those communities specialised groups adopted him as well – apothecaries, bakers, bankers, brewers, coopers, dyers, haberdashers, judges, merchants, murderers, packers, paupers, perfumiers, seedsmen, travellers, thieves, woodturners, unmarried girls . . . and a few more besides! For example, the three bags of gold that he had provided at Patara for the girls' dowries became the money-lending symbol used by the great Lombard merchant bankers: the bags of gold became three golden balls, which is how, in due course, St Nicholas became the patron saint of pawnbrokers.

As quickly as they came, the Normans disappeared, for wherever they settled they integrated and adapted. Just as today children born in the United States to immigrant parents become 100% American in one generation, and by the second have lost almost any identification with their original culture, so it was with the Normans. Within a

single generation they were assimilated by the people among whom they settled. Within two generations, they thought of themselves as French, English, Sicilian, Neapolitan, Russian, even Antiochian – never Norman.

It was perhaps because they had no great cultural heritage of their own that they were so willing to adapt and borrow from others. They were among the most tolerant and understanding patrons of learning the world has ever known. Norman architects were international. Scholars from Europe were encouraged to exchange knowledge with their Arab counterparts, and from the Norman schools emerged some of the greatest intellects of the age.

The very end of the eleventh century saw the beginning of the Crusades, and over the next 200 years people from every country in Europe passed through Bari on their way to and from the Holy Land. There they visited the tomb of St Nicholas and heard the tales of his miraculous deeds. They carried his fame back home with them, and thousands of churches all over Europe were dedicated to him. St Nicholas became the patron saint of Aberdeen, Amsterdam, Apulia, Limerick, Lorraine, Greece, and Russia, and on the River Scheldt near Antwerp a town was named Sint Niklaas.

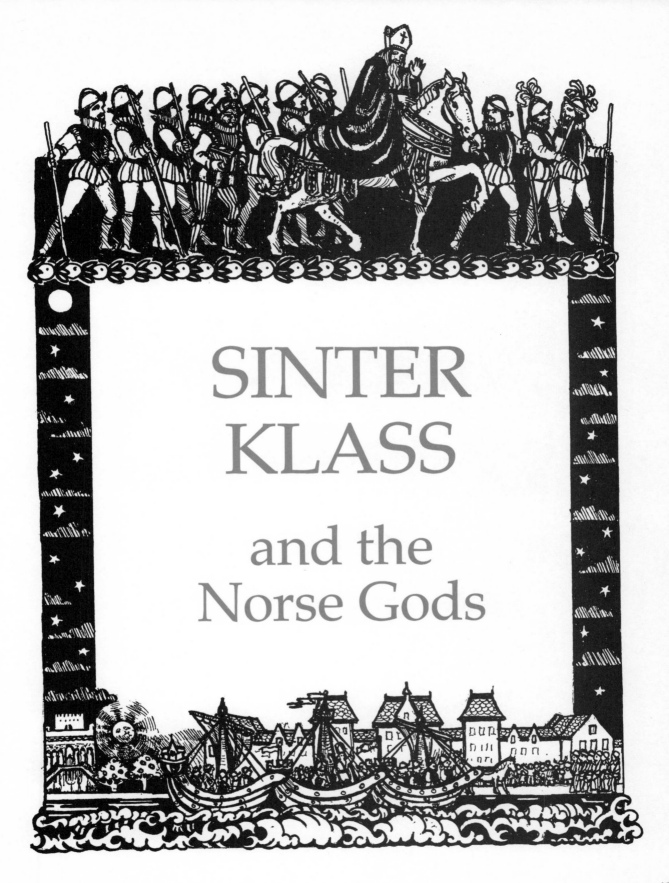

SINTER KLASS

and the
Norse Gods

ituals and beliefs which had once belonged to earlier religions survived as superstitious customs all over Europe, especially in areas beyond the frontiers of the old Roman Empire; the remoter the community, often the stronger the survival. The early Christian missionaries usually demanded only nominal conversion and, in the cause of expediency, it was enough to re-interpret traditional rites and beliefs in terms of Christian values. This is what happened when Kiev was converted in the tenth century and Siberia in the seventeenth. It also happened in Holland.

In 1442 what had been the Norman kingdom of Southern Italy passed to the Spanish kings of Aragon. A few years later the Netherlands also became a Spanish possession. The Dutch ports had long been important trading centres for the North Sea and the Baltic. Now, as Spanish galleons opened up new routes to the Indies and Americas, the Netherlands became the European entrepôt for intercontinental trade. All the key positions in both the administration and the clergy were Spanish appointments. Bishops invariably came from and retired to Spain, and that is why, if you visit Holland and ask about St Nicholas, you will be told in no uncertain terms that his name is Sinter Klaas, that he comes from Spain and dressed as a mediaeval bishop!

According to the Dutch, Sinter Klaas spends most of the year in Spain compiling all the deeds, good and bad, of Dutch children in a big leather-bound ledger. To help him he has a secretary and a little Moorish assistant called Black Peter (Zwart Piet). Spain won the last of her territory from the Arab Caliphs in 1492, so when the Netherlands became part of the Spanish Empire in 1516 a percentage of the Spanish population was still Moorish. Thus it was in keeping with the fashion of the times that St Nicholas should acquire a Moorish servant to help him.

Every year during the second fortnight in November, Sinter Klaas's secretary packs up the big red ledger. Black

Peter loads up the toys and presents, and they all set sail for the Netherlands. The exact date of their arrival varies from year to year, but it is always two or three weeks before St Nicholas's Eve, 5th December.

At Amsterdam their ship brings them and their mediaeval retinue through the canals to the centre of the town, where the Mayor is waiting to greet them. A guard of red-coated musketeers lines the rail. Sinter Klaas in the full regalia of bishop, with mitre, cape and crozier, stands in the bow waving to the crowds. Beside him are Black Peter, in page's costume, and the Secretary holding the big red book.

Sinter Klaas comes ashore and the Mayor makes a speech. Press cameras click while Dutch radio and television commentators describe the scene. It is a national event. A great parade is already lined up but Sinter Klaas delays his departure with a short walk-about, shaking hands with the crowd, and asking the children questions. Eventually Sinter Klaas mounts his white horse and the procession moves off through the streets. There are bands and dancers, carnival characters and commercial floats. Sinter Klaas is preceded by crowds of mediaeval heralds, carrying banners similar to those in Bari. The whole parade stretches for well over a mile.

In the weeks leading up to 5th December, Sinter Klaas and his helpers are extremely busy. During the daytime they visit schools and hospitals and look in on big stores

and restaurants where children welcome them with traditional songs. While Sinter Klaas listens to whispered confessions, Black Peter distributes small presents or, supposedly, the occasional reprimand. For while Sinter Klaas attends to good children, Black Peter has the job of dealing with the bad ones. If children have been naughty he should leave a switch instead of a present so that their parents can give them a beating. If they have been excessively bad he is supposed to carry them off in his sack.

If the daytime is busy, the nights are even busier, for this is when Sinter Klaas rides over the rooftops on his white horse, stopping to listen at the chimneys to check if children are behaving themselves. Before they go to bed, children place a wooden clog beside the fire, filled with hay and carrots for Sinter Klaas's horse. Of course, they can never be sure just which night he is going to call, but in the morning they always know, for if he has stopped by, the hay and carrots will have gone and in their place will be a token present or some sweets.

The main presents are given on Sinter Klaas's Eve. Unlike Christmas presents, they are not wrapped up in pretty paper but each is hidden or disguised in some way. A present may be in the middle of a cake, inside a glove of wet sand, or in a series of boxes of ever decreasing sizes, and it may have been left anywhere in the house from the attic to the cellar. It is always accompanied by a short poem written to embarrass the recipient – perhaps it might refer to a secret love or to a recent mishap. The poems and presents are all anonymous and are simply signed 'Sinter Klaas'. Everyone has to read their poem in a loud voice and finish by saying 'Thank you, Sinter Klaas'. This custom of writing verses to poke fun at people is not just confined to the home. In the days leading up to December 5th everyone is at it – at school, at work, on television, in the newspapers, even in parliament. It is a national pastime.

The giving of gifts on St Nicholas's Eve was first

recorded in Central France, where early in the 12th century nuns went out secretly at night to leave gifts of Spanish oranges, nuts, or fruit at the homes of the poor. From France the custom spread to the rest of Europe.

The present customs in Holland probably had their origin in the 13th and 14th centuries. In churches dedicated to Sint Niklaas the choirboys would be given pocket money and a holiday to celebrate the Saint's feast day. In church schools this gradually developed into a custom where one of the masters would don a long white beard and, dressed up as the Bishop, would reward or punish the pupils for their year's work. Gradually the tradition passed from the schools into people's homes.

Many of the customs surrounding Sinter Klaas are vestiges of an older, pre-Christian religion. Checking up on naughty children, riding a white horse, and leaving food out at night, can all be traced back to Woden or Odin, the greatest and wisest of all the old Norse Gods. He too had a long white beard and spent the year in a distant

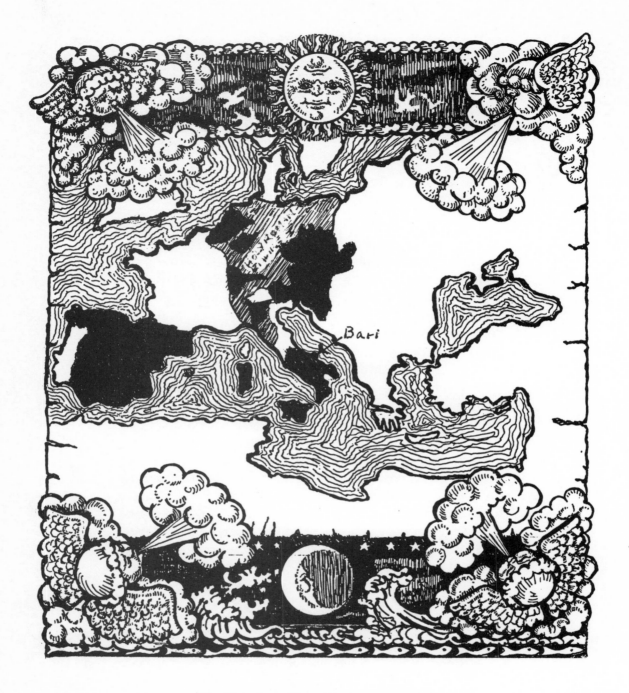

The Hapsburg Empire circa 1556 AD

land, Valhalla, where he lived with the spirits of the great Viking heroes. On the night of the winter solstice, 21st December, they would all come back to Earth to seek out evil-doers. Odin himself would lead the hunt on his great white horse, carrying off naughty children in a howl of wind. For many centuries after the coming of Christianity, people in the Netherlands continued to leave out offerings of grain for Odin's horse and food for the spirits.

But the traditions of Odin are even stronger in Scandinavia. In Finland, at one time, gifts were given anonymously, thrown through an open window as St Nicholas had done with the bags of gold. But gradually St Nicholas assumed human form, adopting the older name of *Joulupukki* which literally means Yule Goat and again harks back to Odin and the old Norse customs.

The earliest inhabitants of what is now Norway and Sweden were a race of cattle herders – a small, dark

people. In due course they were followed by a new wave of settlers who were farmers. As the newcomers moved in, they enclosed the open grazing lands, forcing the original cattle herders to seek refuge in the more inaccessible areas. Hiding out in swamps, on the islands and among the tundra of the far North, they went underground, living in caves and subterranean dwellings. They learned the art of camouflage and developed the skill of moving quickly to avoid detection. Long after the original inhabitants died out, their fame remained. In Norway they were known as the Nisser, in Sweden the Tomtar.

These were the Little People, who inspired a superstitious and often justified fear in the Norse incomers. Their skills of survival were interpreted as supernatural abilities of appearing and disappearing at will, levitating, changing shape, and being swallowed up by the earth. Their contact with the Norsemen was essentially mischievous and sometimes vindictive. They caused sickness and ruined the crops, buildings caught fire, animals died, and children were stolen from their cots. If a farmer moved, the Little People stayed with his herds and the bad luck continued. The Little People could not be eradicated. But over the years, an unspoken pact gradually developed. The farmer would placate the Little People by leaving out small gifts of food. In return, the Little People would cease their mischief and use their skills to further the fortunes of the farm. Each race became mutually dependent on the other.

As the old Norse religion was replaced with Christianity, so the old beliefs – and the Little People with them – were relegated to the realms of superstition. But nowadays the bringer of gifts at Christmas is a tiny Yule goblin, the Chief of the Little People. In Sweden, he is known as the *Jultomte*, in Iceland as the *Jola Sveinar*, and in Norway and Denmark they call him the *Julenisse*, Nisse being the old form of Nils or Nicholas. With his little pointed cap, dressed all in red, he comes every year and children leave out a plate of porridge to keep him in a good humour.

FATHER CHRISTMAS

The Pagan Entertainer

Perhaps the country where the vestiges of old pagan beliefs and customs remain most visibly part of Christmas is England.

As in the rest of Europe, St Nicholas had made his way to England, and by 1400 there were over a thousand churches consecrated to him. The English have a carol dating from about this time:

> *I saw three ships come sailing by,*
> *Come sailing by, come sailing by,*
> *I saw three ships come sailing by,*
> *On Christmas Day in the morning.*

Were these the three ships which carried St Nicholas from Myra to Bari? If so, it was perhaps in England that St Nicholas first became associated with Christmas.

He certainly figured largely in the Feast of Fools, an end-of-the-year festival which had its origins in the old Roman celebration of Saturnalia. The Roman Saturn was the God of Peace and Plenty, and for the period of his festival everyone became equal. The established order was turned upside down: men dressed as women; masters waited on their slaves. It was a time of extravagance and excess. For the duration of the holiday a 'king' was elected to act as master of ceremonies – making his own laws and enforcing the most ridiculous whims.

Long after the Romans, Saturnalia persisted as part of the mid-winter celebrations in many parts of Europe – particularly France and Germany. In England the Feast of Fools was presided over by an elected Lord of Misrule; in Scotland he was called the Abbot of Unreason. The world went topsy turvy. People wore masks and dressed up in costume, in much the same way as modern-day guisers at Halloween in Scotland. Men dressed as women and masters waited on their servants – just as in Roman times – a tradition which is still carried on in the British army when the officers serve the men at Christmas lunch. The Lord of Misrule would even lead his 'court' into church and disrupt the service. They would make a burlesque of the liturgy, reading prayer books upside down through orange peel spectacles, playing pipes and drums, dancing in the pews, riding hobby horses down the aisles and letting off fire-crackers under the pulpit.

The clergy too joined in the spirit of the festival by electing a boy bishop from the choir. He was chosen on St Nicholas's Eve to commemorate the original boy Bishop of Myra, and until he delivered his sermon on Innocents' Day (28th December) he assumed the full role of Bishop. He could appoint his friends as canons and priests and

wear full episcopal regalia. His blessing was greatly valued, and he and his retinue would be welcomed and feasted throughout the diocese. In Salisbury Cathedral there is actually a tomb of a chorister who died during his period of office and it seems he was buried with the full funerary honours of a real bishop.

Alongside St Nicholas and the Boy Bishop was the flush-faced, holly-crowned Master of Ceremonies of the Festive Season – Old Father Christmas. The very title 'Old' reflects his ancient origins. Like Sinter Klaas he inherited Odin's long white beard; he traditionally travelled mounted on a white donkey or even a horned goat.

In the Middle Ages Father Christmas presided over the Mummers, a group of travelling players who wandered from tavern to tavern, and village to village. In a few remote communities the tradition still survives. There can be up to a dozen players. The costumes are made by turning clothes inside out and sewing on strips of torn cloth, and the players are all disguised with blackened faces. Many of them wear complete masks or head-dresses with ribbons hanging down to hide their faces. The players must not be recognised as real people for in origin they are men of magic, and, if it is to succeed, magic has to be anonymous.

Their play incorporates many elements derived from pagan ritual. The details of the plot vary from village to village, for until fairly recently the words were never written down. They were simply passed on from generation to generation and modified over the centuries to include topical references. But the central theme is always the same: the continuity of life.

In the Cotswolds a version of this play is still performed by the Waterleigh Bottom players.

Old Father Christmas is the Master of Ceremonies, the high priest of the proceedings, who links the whole performance together and introduces the characters.

First he presents the Hero – King George, 'a man of courage bold' who throws out a challenge to the villain. In different versions of the play the villain is sometimes a Fiery Dragon, sometimes a Turk (reflecting their threat to Europe after the collapse of the Byzantine Empire), or sometimes an even more modern bogeyman like Bonaparte or Hitler.

King George first fights the dragon:

and then goes on to challenge Bonaparte. But when Bonaparte falls, mortally wounded, Father Christmas bursts into tears:

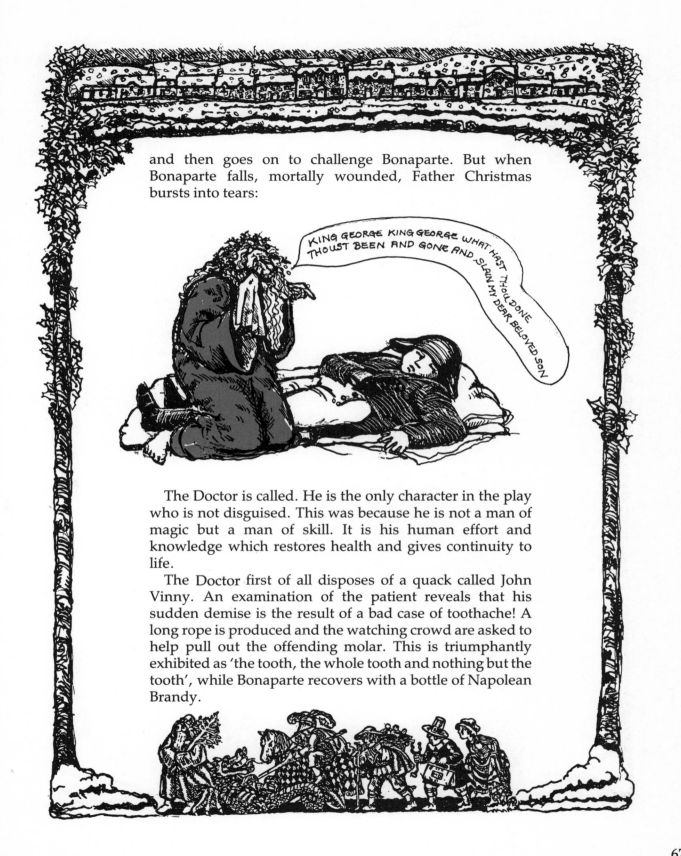

KING GEORGE KING GEORGE WHAT HAST THOU DONE THOUST BEEN AND GONE AND SLAIN MY DEAR BELOVED SON

The Doctor is called. He is the only character in the play who is not disguised. This was because he is not a man of magic but a man of skill. It is his human effort and knowledge which restores health and gives continuity to life.

The Doctor first of all disposes of a quack called John Vinny. An examination of the patient reveals that his sudden demise is the result of a bad case of toothache! A long rope is produced and the watching crowd are asked to help pull out the offending molar. This is triumphantly exhibited as 'the tooth, the whole tooth and nothing but the tooth', while Bonaparte recovers with a bottle of Napolean Brandy.

This idea of bringing a dead man back to life can be traced back to pre-Christian times when, at the midwinter solstice, the God of the Old Year was ritually slain to allow Life to be reborn in the God of the Year to Come.

This is really the end of the story. From here on the play becomes totally obscure as the rest of the characters simply come on, say a few lines about who they are, and go off. It seems that, although these players must have had parts once upon a time, their original roles have been forgotten as new characters have been introduced, and now they just exist as characters.

One of the characters is Saucy Jack. He has a rather macabre collection of dolls strapped to his back, and an unintelligible riddle:

Did he perhaps once have the role of the villain, now played by Bonaparte? Or are his origins much earlier, with his doll effigies reflecting a form of sacrifice practiced by the celts and described by Roman writers, when human and animal victims were burned alive inside a huge wickerwork effigy of a man?

Alongside him are other apparently irrelevant characters. There is Niddy Noddy who is

ALL HEAD AND NO BODY
ALL FEET AND NO TOES
GIVE US SOME MONEY OR OUT I GOES
TIS MONEY I WANT TIS MONEY I GRAVE
SO GIVE US A GROAT OR I'LL DANCE
ON YOUR GRAVE

Mary Tinker is the sort of character who would have featured large in the Feast of Fools, a man dressed up as a woman (the original pantomime dame), 'a strong wine, ale and beer drinker' who is padded out to appear enormously fat and who claims to play the hurdy gurdy. Beelzebub is more like mediaeval fool than our concept of the Devil:

WITH MY BIG HEAD AND LITTLE WIT
I'M THE JOLLIEST FELLA THATS EVER BEEN HIT
MY HEADS SO LARGE AND MY WIT BE SO SMALL
I'LL SING EE A SONG TO PLEASE EE ALL

Throughout the performance there is one character who wears a white cloak and an ox skull on his head. He never speaks, but mingles with the crowd, snapping his jaws and frightening the children.

The performance ends with all the cast singing a traditional Wassail song, while Father Christmas makes a collection

No-one knows how old the mummers' plays really are. But they must rank among the longest running shows on earth, and as an oral tradition their origins may well date back to pre-Roman times.

In the days when Britain was still a land of great forests, trees and animals were important in both the economy and the religion of the Celtic inhabitants. In 601 the Pope wrote to St Augustine in Canterbury, instructing him to adapt the pagan custom of decorating temples with greenery by decking Christian churches in the same manner. The only banned plant was mistletoe because of its importance in the old Celtic religion.

Mistletoe was believed to have amazing medicinal properties. It was a remedy against all poison. It brought
fertility and early childbirth, cured epilepsy, healed ulcers
and many other ills. Pliny described a sacrificial rite based
on the cutting of mistletoe from an oak tree. On the sixth
day of the moon, a druid climbed the tree and cut the
mistletoe with a gold-coloured sickle. The branch was
caught in a white cloth so that it would be untouched by
human hand and two white bulls were sacrificed. These
white cattle with their black tipped horns were the
indigenous British breed that was common until the
Middle Ages and still exist in herds at Chillingham in

Northumberland and Lennoxlove in Lothian. They are small, (the cows weigh about 7 cwt) and are surprisingly agile. They have been known to make a standing jump of six feet!

In many ways, the Druids of Celtic Britain were probably not dissimilar to the more recent Shamans in the Arctic. They did not live in settled communities, but travelled the countryside. Like the Shamans, they were more than just priests. They were also healers, jurists, soothsayers and bards who spent their lifetime learning and passing on oral traditions; a custom still practised in Gaeldom as late as the early eighteenth century. There are pictures of Shamans in Siberia and Lapland wearing reindeer skulls on their heads. Is it so unlikely that the Celtic diviners, or medicine men, might not have worn an ox skull in their ceremonies? There is even a special word in Gaelic for a seer who stands under a waterfall wearing an ox's hide! The sinister ox-headed figure of the mummers' play is surely a distant folk memory of the rituals of the early Celts.

When the Romans arrived in England, the Celtic people were forced to change their ways. The Roman system of administration depended on the centralisation of religion and government. The itinerant ways of the Druids were totally alien to the Roman concept of administration. So priests and jurists became institutionalised in temples and court-houses and the Celtic Gods became Romanised. Only the Bards continued their nomadic way of life, keeping alive a folk-memory of the past. Are the obscure characters who still linger on the fringes of the English mummers' plays perhaps a last link with that oral tradition?

By the Middle Ages, the English Christmas was a curious blend of Celtic, Roman and Christian folklore. In *Marmion* Sir Walter Scott describes a scene in a Scottish Border castle in the early sixteenth century:

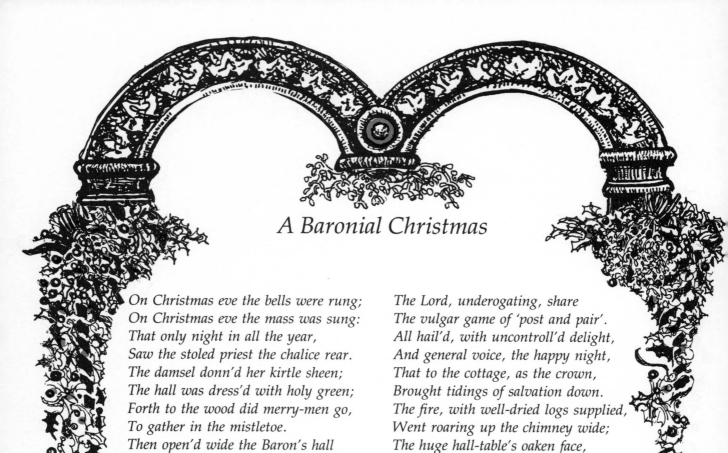

A Baronial Christmas

On Christmas eve the bells were rung;
On Christmas eve the mass was sung:
That only night in all the year,
Saw the stoled priest the chalice rear.
The damsel donn'd her kirtle sheen;
The hall was dress'd with holy green;
Forth to the wood did merry-men go,
To gather in the mistletoe.
Then open'd wide the Baron's hall
To vassal, tenant, serf, and all;
Power laid his rod of rule aside,
And Ceremony doff'd his pride.
The heir, with roses in his shoes,
That night might village partner choose.

The Lord, underogating, share
The vulgar game of 'post and pair'.
All hail'd, with uncontroll'd delight,
And general voice, the happy night,
That to the cottage, as the crown,
Brought tidings of salvation down.
The fire, with well-dried logs supplied,
Went roaring up the chimney wide;
The huge hall-table's oaken face,
Scrubb'd till it shone, the day to grace,
Bore then upon its massive board
No mark to part the squire and lord.
Then was brought in the lusty brawn,
By old blue-coated serving-man;

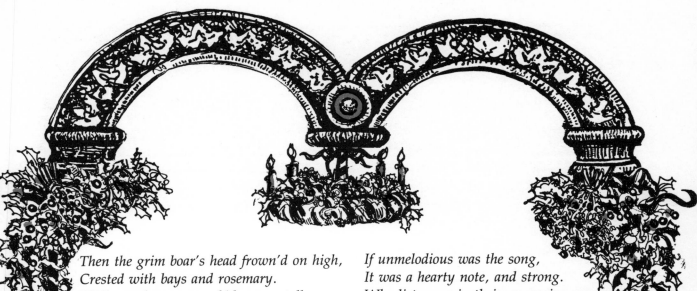

Then the grim boar's head frown'd on high,
Crested with bays and rosemary.
Well can the green-garb'd ranger tell,
How, when, and where, the monster fell;
What dogs before his death he tore,
And all the baiting of the boar.
The wassel round, in good brown bowls,
Garnish'd with ribbons, blithely trowels.
There the huge sirloin reek'd; hard by
Plumb-porridge stood, and Christmas pie;
Or fail'd old Scotland to produce,
At such high tide, her savoury goose.
Then came the merry maskers In,
And carols roar'd with blithesome din;

If unmelodious was the song,
It was a hearty note, and strong.
Who lists may in their mumming see
Traces of ancient mystery;
White shirts supplied the masquerade,
And smutted cheeks the visors made;
But, O! what maskers, richly dight,
Can boast of bosoms half so light!
England was merry England, when
Old Christmas brought his sports again.
'Twas Christmas broach'd the mightiest ale,
'Twas Christmas told the merriest tale;
A Christmas gambol oft could cheer
The poor man's heart through half the year.

At the Reformation, these Saints and Saints' days were violently attacked by the Protestants and, by the second half of the sixteenth century, had entirely died out. St Nicholas and the Christ Mass were no exception. In the Puritan strongholds of Europe, Christmas, like all the other traditional Catholic festivals, was finally abolished.

In some places abolition was more permanent than in others. In Scotland, John Knox put an end to Christmas in 1562 and although it was proclaimed a bank holiday in 1871, it is only recently that it has really been celebrated in any meaningful way. In England, the Puritans came to power with Oliver Cromwell. At first their ordinances were mainly concerned with banning plays, but this gradually extended to an attack on the whole of Christmas. By 1647 Christmas was only surviving at Oxford *amid a world of skullbreaking* and at Ipswich *with some loss of life*. Eventually, in 1652, the holiday was officially banned altogether, and although it came back eight years later with the restoration of the monarchy, many of the old customs were never revived.

Throughout Protestant Europe, St Nicholas was secularised.

In Holland, Sint Niklaas became the vernacular Sinter Klaas and while he kept the mediaeval garb of a bishop complete with mitre and crozier, he became a figure of fun – a folk character with no religious connotations.

In Northern Germany, the Lutherans were not so extreme and, while St Nicholas' Eve itself disappeared, in many places the giving of gifts and the other customs associated with it were transferred to the night before Christmas. St Nicholas was stripped of his episcopal robes and dressed instead in furs with a cap to match. He also

lost his religious title. In some places he became known as *Pelze Nicol* (Furry Nick), in others he was the *Weihnachtsmann* (the Christmas Man) or even *Schimmelreiter* (the rider of the white horse), a throwback once again to Odin.

In other areas, the Protestants invented *Christkindl*, a Christ child figure often played by a girl in a white robe with a veil and a star on her head – another legacy from the Roman Festivals.

The German Gift Giver had a fur-clad assistant *Knecht Ruprecht* – armed with a switch for beating naughty children and a sack and chains for carrying off really bad ones. By the end of the seventeenth century, these characters had many different names. In Schleswig Holstein there was *Rubbert* or *Rower*; in Mecklenberg and Pommerania *Rugeklas*, *Bulleklas*, and *Sumerklas*; in Brandeburg *Pelznickel*, in Thuringia *Herscheklos*, in Bohemia *Ruprich*, in Eastern Austria *Bartel*; in Switzerland *Sammichlaus* to name just a few! Local traditions varied slightly but most horrific of all was the Austrian *Krampus* with a long red tongue

and wild demonic eyes who roamed the dark nights looking for bad children.

In countries like Hungary, where Protestantism was subsequently replaced by a restoration of Catholicism, the religious St Nicholas, the secular Christkindl, and the Weihnachtsmann traditions all exist side by side.

In Russia, a descendant of Nikolai Chudovorits appeared – Father Frost. His home is in the land of the Shamans, far beyond the Arctic Circle. He arrives in Russia on New Year's Day, accompanied by his daughter, the Snow Maiden. She helps him deliver the presents and place them under the trees which are brought into every home for the festival. They come on a reindeer sledge. He is dressed all in furs and has a long white beard and long white hair. The Snow Maiden, like the *Christkindl*, is all in white and carries a glittering wand.

In Poland, St Nicholas still comes on the 6th December with his presents: on Christmas Eve an unseen angel delivers more presents and finally in January, Father Frost arrives for a third round of gift-giving. In France, the St Nicholas tradition also largely transferred to the night before Christmas. *Père Noel* (Father Christmas) replaced St Nicholas to look after the good children, and *Père Fouettard* (Father Spanker) was introduced around about 1700 to deal with the naughty ones.

In North America, New England was settled by Puritans. In 1651, taking their example from their Cromwellian counterparts in the Old World, they introduced a law making the celebration of Christmas a fineable offence. The law was rescinded thirty years later but many New Englanders never celebrated Christmas as a holiday again until the present century.

Further to the south, on an island called Manhattan, the Dutch had bartered trinkets with local Indians for land. In 1626 a fleet of ships arrived with the first settlers from

Holland. With them, as figurehead on the flagship, came
Sinter Klaas and in due course a gilded statue of him was
erected in the main square. They called their small settlement Nieuw Amsterdam. Nearly forty years later, the
British took over and renamed the place New York. The
Dutch stayed on and their celebration of St Nicholas' Eve
continued unchanged, except that in the century that
followed Sinter Klaas gradually became anglicised to Santa
Claus. And it was in New York, in December 1822, that
the Santa Claus we know was born.

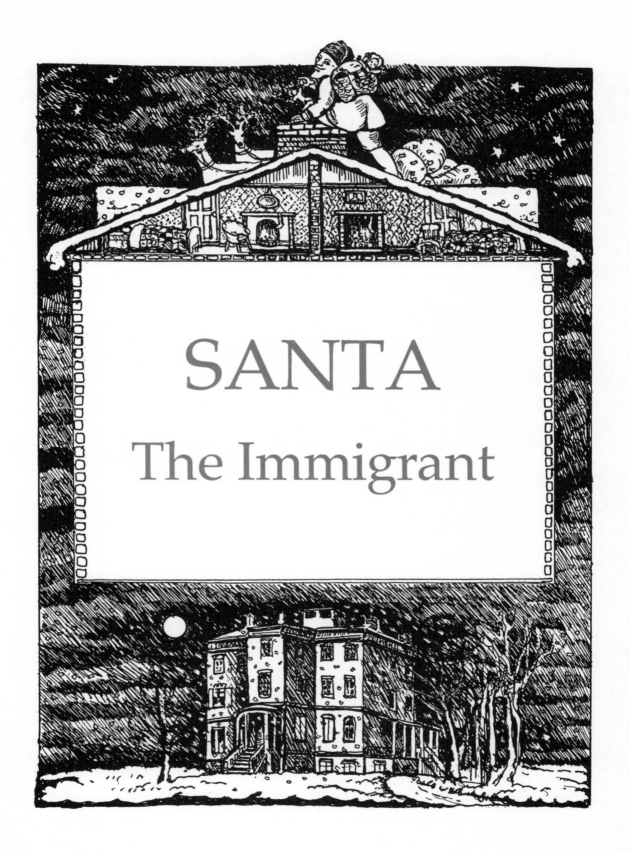

SANTA

The Immigrant

In 1822, New York was a large colonial town of wooden houses and cobbled streets. The tallest buildings then were windmills and church steeples. The town was clustered round the southern tip of Manhattan. Further north was open country and large estates. One of the estates was called Chelsea. Today it is a district between 8th and 10th Avenues and bounded by West 19th and 24th Streets, but then it was 94 acres of open parkland with an imposing mansion overlooking the Hudson River – the home of Professor Clement Clark Moore.

The house had originally been built by his grandfather. Clement Clark Moore had been born there, and now he had six children of his own who ranged from seven years old to eight months. Every day he drove into town to teach Oriental and Greek Literature at the General Theological Seminary.

As a writer, he was best known for his Hebrew dictionary but privately he also wrote little rhymes to entertain his wife and children on special occasions. He was no great poet but his verses amused the family.

It was Christmas Eve and New York lay under a mantle of snow. That afternoon, Professor Moore set off by horse-drawn sleigh to buy the Christmas turkey. Washington Market was at the southernmost point of Manhattan and it was a good hour's drive to get there and another hour to come back. He had spent the morning helping Jan, his odd job man, to clear snow off the paths round the house. Jan was of Dutch descent, a tubby little man with a white beard, twinkling eyes and rosy cheeks. An idea for a poem began to take shape, as the jingle of sleighbells and the horses' hooves pounded out a rhythm on the snow.

That evening when the Moore family gathered round the fireside, Professor Moore read it for the first time.

 ## A Visit From Saint Nicholas

'Twas the night before Christmas, when all through the house
Not a creature was stirring, not even a mouse;
The stockings were hung by the chimney with care,
In hopes that St Nicholas soon would be there;
The children were nestled all snug in their beds,
While visions of sugar-plums danced in their heads;
And Mamma in her 'kerchief, and I in my cap
Had just settled our brains for a long winter's nap;
When out on the lawn there arose such a clatter,
I sprang from the bed to see what was the matter,
Away to the window I flew like a flash,
Tore open the shutters and threw up the sash.
The moon on the breast of the new-fallen snow,
Gave the lustre of mid-day to objects below,
When, what to my wondering eyes should appear,
But a miniature sleigh, and eight tiny reindeer,
With a little old driver, so lively and quick,
I knew in a moment it must be St Nick.
More rapid than eagles his coursers they came,
And he whistled, and shouted, and called them by name: "Now,
Dasher! now Dancer! now Prancer and Vixen!
On, Comet! on, cupid! on, Donder and Blitzen!
To the top of the porch! to the top of the wall!
Now dash away! dash away! dash away all!"
As dry leaves that before the wild hurricane fly,
When they meet with an obstacle, mount to the sky;
So up to the house-top the coursers they flew,
With the sleigh full of toys, and St Nicholas too.
And then in a twinkling, I heard on the roof,

The prancing and pawing of each little hoof,
As I drew in my head, and was turning around,
Down the chimney St Nicholas came with a bound.
He was dressed all in fur, from his head to his foot,
And his clothes were all tarnished with ashes and soot;
A bundle of toys he had flung on his back,
And he looked like a pedlar just opening his pack.
His eyes – how they twinkled! his dimples, how merry!
His cheeks were like roses, his nose like a cherry!
His droll little mouth was drawn up like a bow,

And the beard of his chin was as white as the snow;
The stump of a pipe he held tight in his teeth,
And the smoke it encircled his head like a wreath;
He had a broad face and a little round belly,
That shook when he laughed, like a bowlful of jelly.
He was chubby and plump, a right jolly old elf,
And I laughed when I saw him, in spite of myself;
A wink of his eye and a twist of his head,
Soon gave me to know I had nothing to dread.
He spoke not a word, but went straight to his work,
And fill'd all the stockings; then turned with a jerk,
And laying his finger aside of his nose,
And giving a nod, up the chimney he rose;
He sprang to his sleigh, to his team gave a whistle,
And away they all flew like the down of a thistle.
But I heard him exclaim, ere he drove out of sight,
'Happy Christmas to all and to all a good night'.

The children loved it. 'Read it again, Daddy,' they cried. Over Christmas it was recited to relatives. The relatives copied it to read to their friends, who in turn copied it for others. Eventually it reached a Sunday School teacher who kept it and read it to her class the following December. The children's response was so enthusiastic that, without a second thought, she sent it to the local newspaper.

On 23rd December 1823 the verses appeared in the *Troy Sentinel*, with a statement by the editor to the effect that he had no idea of the identity of the author. Of course news of the publication eventually got back to Clement Clark Moore, but with a reputation to preserve as an author of scholarly and theological works, he was so embarrassed that for fifteen years he refused to acknowledge the poem as his. By then it had become a national favourite.

Professor Moore's poem was reprinted many times. Illustrators set to work, in particular Thomas Nast who produced a series of black and white drawings for *Harpers Illustrated Weekly*, which immediately caught people's imagination. Although his basic character originated in the old Dutch Sinter Klaas, Professor Moore's Santa Claus incorporated characteristics from many other European cultures. It was an artist of German extraction who, remembering the Weihnachtsman of his childhood, first gave Santa his red, fur-trimmed costume. Scandinavia gave him his small stature which enabled him to slip down the chimney, which together with his flying sledge and magic reindeer, he inherited from Russia. Santa Claus personified the great American dream, the melting pot of Old World cultures that was the making of the New. The spotlight was on. As America's first showbusiness ambassador, he was all set to capture the world with a dream.

Meanwhile, in England, Christmas had never really recovered from being banned by Oliver Cromwell and the Puritans. It had come back into the calendar but was only a shadow of the great festival it used to be.

When Queen Victoria came to the throne in 1837, Britain was moving into an age of prosperity greater than she had ever known. More and more, the map of the world was being coloured pink. As new territories came under British rule, they brought with them new markets and greater resources for British industry. It was a time of opportunity when living standards and social conditions were rapidly improving. In the towns a bigger middle-class was emerging – a literate class with money and leisure, but unsure of its place within the traditional framework of British society. Social acceptability was all important, and what better models of correctness and moral rectitude than Queen Victoria and Prince Albert?

The daily doings of the royal family were followed as closely as any modern soap opera, for this was the Age of the Magazine. New printing techniques had resulted in a sudden growth of specialist journals to both entertain and inform. For a class out to better itself, they were the manuals of etiquette and fashion, and they played a major part in the re-invention of the English Christmas.

See that there is abundance of Christmas literature about. Servants and children as well as the grown-up guests delight in looking at pictures. A pretty well written story of Christmas happiness is wont to diffuse a sense of enjoyment among its readers.

The magazines responded to people's need for a season of escapism from the humdrum of industrialised city life. The new English middle class had the money and the time to enjoy their leisure, and there was a great nostalgia to rediscover the spirit of the simple rural Christmases of yesteryear.

The one ingredient to be universally infused is gladness. Everybody can, at all events, endeavour to bring goodwill and a smiling countenance to the festive board, banishing for a time the recollection of everyday worries. There is all the rest of the year to think of them. This is peculiarly the children's time and we would have them as happy as we were in the old Christmas Days of long ago.

Prince Albert himself was one of the great authorities for

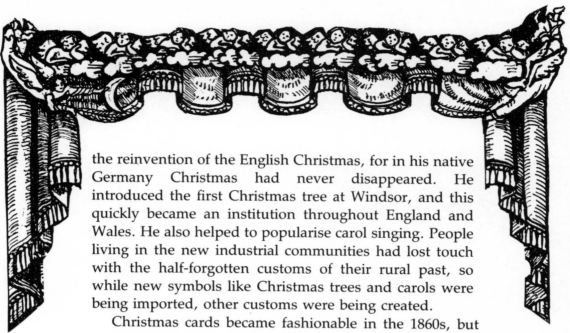

the reinvention of the English Christmas, for in his native Germany Christmas had never disappeared. He introduced the first Christmas tree at Windsor, and this quickly became an institution throughout England and Wales. He also helped to popularise carol singing. People living in the new industrial communities had lost touch with the half-forgotten customs of their rural past, so while new symbols like Christmas trees and carols were being imported, other customs were being created.

Christmas cards became fashionable in the 1860s, but not everyone approved. *Punch* announced, 'I hate those redbreasts,' and a few years later *The Times* declared Christmas cards 'a social evil'. By 1888 chaos in the mail service had reached such a peak that the Post Office was forced to start its first 'Post Early' campaign. Magazines were full of articles about the growing commercialisation of Christmas and the growth of a new industry manufacturing cards and crackers. They gave suggestions of presents to buy, dishes to cook, games to play – even how to decorate your house:

> *It is worthwhile to bestow some little trouble on the decoration of the rooms. Have plenty of shining holly, and laurel too, and don't omit the mistletoe, for we have long ago forgotten all about the paganism, magic and superstition which surrounded it.*

There was no general tradition of hanging up stockings or expecting a visit down the chimney. Even as late as the 1880s there was no established way of giving presents.

> *Presents are inseparably connected with the season. . . .*
> *There are two points to be considered – first, what to give,*
> *and then how best to make the giving a source of pleasure*

Suggestions included making a Christmas ship about two feet long with alum crystallised in the rigging to look like snow and the present concealed in the hold. Alternatively you could put the presents inside a giant snowball made of calico and wadding, about a yard in circumference, which would burst open. Another idea was a gypsy-tent rigged up in a back drawing-room with a presiding gypsy to distribute the presents or a post-office or parcels delivery office manned by a bustling official.

On the quest for nostalgia, popular novelists and particularly Charles Dickens also played a major role, with descriptions of the idealised Christmas at Dingly Dell and

Bob Cratchit's Christmas dinner. His *Christmas Carol* repopularised the pagan character of Old Father Christmas,

> *clothed in one single green robe or mantle, bordered with white fur. The garment hung so loosely on the figure, that its capacious breast was bare, as if disdaining to be warded or concealed by any artifice. Its feet, observable beneath the angle folds of the garment, were also bare, and on its head it wore no other covering than a holly wreath, set here and there with shining circles.*

Father Christmas also made a theatrical comeback, appearing in the 1840s at Drury Lane in an adaptation of the old mummers' play. The Saturnalian tradition of a man dressed as a woman re-emerged in that indispensable character, the Pantomime Dame.

When Clement Clark Moore's poem was first published in England, Santa Claus had made quite an impact, but as a gift-giver he was only one of a number of rival claimants. The magazines of the day were full of alternative suggestions: Cheap Jack, a survivor of the mummers' plays, The Lord of Misrule, the German Knecht Rupert, and Father Christmas himself . . . Santa Claus by no means held the centre stage in Victorian England.

SAINT NICHOLAS

The Survivor

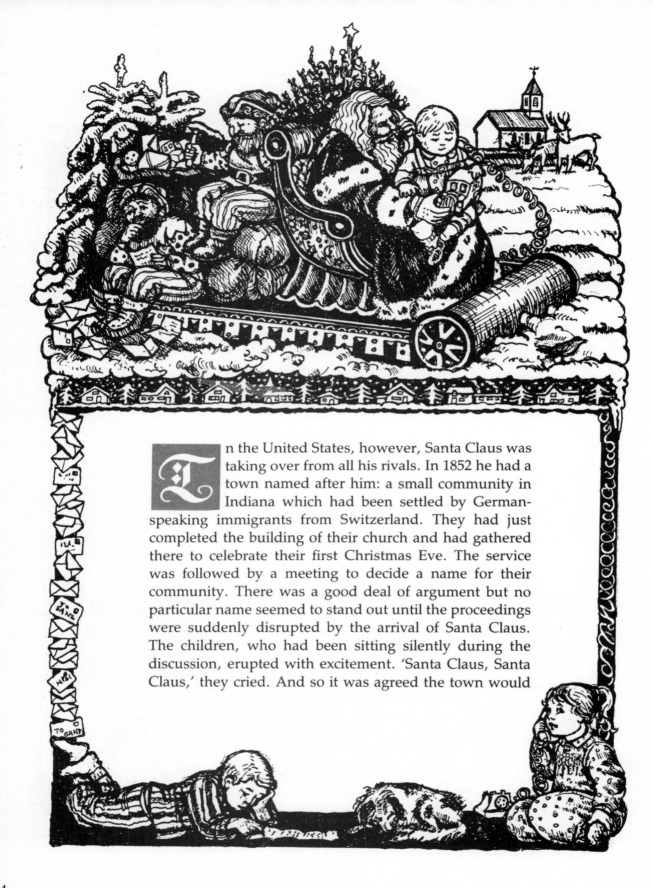

In the United States, however, Santa Claus was taking over from all his rivals. In 1852 he had a town named after him: a small community in Indiana which had been settled by German-speaking immigrants from Switzerland. They had just completed the building of their church and had gathered there to celebrate their first Christmas Eve. The service was followed by a meeting to decide a name for their community. There was a good deal of argument but no particular name seemed to stand out until the proceedings were suddenly disrupted by the arrival of Santa Claus. The children, who had been sitting silently during the discussion, erupted with excitement. 'Santa Claus, Santa Claus,' they cried. And so it was agreed the town would

be known as Santa Claus.

In due course a post office was established and the little community continued, virtually unnoticed by the outside world, until during the First World War letters addressed to Santa Claus started arriving. The Postmaster wrote replies and in the 1920s the whole story was publicised in a national cartoon. The number of children's letters to Santa Claus increased so dramatically that the Postmaster simply could not cope. So the authorities in Washington decided to solve the problem by closing down the post office altogether. There was an enormous outcry. Local individuals and organisations offered to come in and help reply to the children's letters. In the end Washington reluctantly gave in but ruled that there would never be another Santa Claus Post Office in the United States.

And today the tradition continues.

> *Dear Santa,*
> *We live in Minnesota. Our name is on the mailbox. You go straight down, then you go left and then right and then, straight up ahead. Our house is all white with green trim on it, but please Santa do not put another frozen frankfurter in my stocking this year.*
> *Mary Jo.*

Every letter gets answered – almost 15,000 every year, and in addition there are a further million letters mailed for individuals and companies who simply want the post mark.

Of course everything in the town has the name Santa Claus. There's a Santa Claus Cemetery, a Santa Claus

Sheriff, a Santa Claus Boiler Company, and even a Santa Claus Fire Department, equipped with a tender called Rudolph with a large red light glowing on the 'nose' of its engine!

All over the United States, entrepreneurs have tried to jump on the commercial bandwagon. One of the most disastrous attempts is another town called Santa Claus – built in Arizona in 1937 as a tourist attraction in the middle of the desert – resident population, four! The curious thing is that this monument to bad taste has survived for the best part of fifty years.

It was Coca Cola who really exploited Santa's commercial potential. At Christmas in 1931 Santa Claus was shown swigging from a bottle of Coca Cola on billboards, in magazines, and on shop counters all over the States. Wherever Coca Cola was being sold in the world, Santa Claus was there to promote it, and continued to do so every Christmas for the next thirty-five years. But this Santa was different from the small gnome-like character in Nast's drawings. Now Santa was an all-American male, big and strong and six feet tall.

In 1949 a bright businessman had the idea of naming a settlement in Upper New York State 'North Pole' and

starting the first theme park in the United States with its own North Pole Post Office. The North Pole itself is a refrigerated rod outside Santa's House. The village is open for most of the year and employs several Santas, all of whom have grown real beards and long white hair. The actors identify increasingly with the part and in time some have even come to believe that they really are Santa Claus. In two instances men have gone as far as legally changing their names. Once a man is convinced that he is Santa Claus, it becomes increasingly difficult to live alongside anyone else with a similar conviction, so the village is not without internal tensions.

Although North Pole was the first Santa theme park, now there are many others all over the United States. But it is in a department store during the weeks leading up to Christmas that American children are most likely to encounter Santa Claus.

Being a Store Santa is not always as easy as it might at first appear. Children can easily get over-excited and Santa can regularly find his knee is warm and wet. That is when he remembers he has to go and feed his reindeer! On occasion Santa may even be physically attacked. Usually this takes the form of a well delivered kick on the

shin, but it can be worse. On one occasion in Los Angeles a little boy marched in and hit a Santa over the head with a heavy metal toy, literally splitting his skull open. In spite of the blood pouring down his forhead, he kept his smile fixed on his face and gently asked the little fellow why he had done it. 'You didn't give me what I asked for last year!' was the outraged reply.

The Santa photograph is a major part of the job. Usually this is the department store's way of offsetting costs. But in the United States, Santa poses not just with children: adults appear with a whole range of child substitutes from beribboned poodles to pet pythons!

Every Christmas, Macy's, the New York department store, organises a big street parade. A few years ago, as the procession was being televised nationwide, Santa rose from his throne to wave to the children. A great cheer went up from the crowd and his trousers dropped round his knees. It was a classic incident which is regularly quoted by one of America's largest employment agencies which runs the University of Santa Claus, a professional training school which awards a 'BSc' qualification – Bachelor of Santa Clausery!

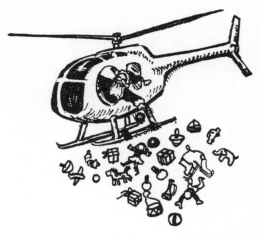

The transformation in character simply by donning a costume can be quite remarkable. With the English mummers it was said that to reveal the identity beneath the disguise would break the magic. In all primitive religions when a player dons a mask he is deemed no longer an ordinary man. For himself and those who take part in the ritual, he embodies the spirit he is impersonating. Equally, for a man in a Santa suit, the disguise is so complete that he ceases to be himself. He feels different and people treat him differently. Who gives a thought to the real person beneath the whiskers and the wig? He *is* Santa Claus.

Although Santa Claus started out in the USA as the gift-giver, it was a short step to charity collector. And it is now a common sight to see a Santa Claus ringing his handbell on a street corner and rattling a collecting tin.

The money may go to a good cause. Alternatively it may just end up in Santa's pocket. Anyone can rent a costume and not all Santas are honest. The disguise is a perfect cover for petty crime. If you are a burglar and the children surprise you, you simply tell them to be good and go back to sleep. When all the silver is found missing the following

morning, who is going to pick you out in an identity parade? Alternatively there is shoplifting. Santa goes into the store with his sack half-empty and comes out with it full. No uniformed figure of authority wants to be seen interrogating, let alone apprehending, Santa Claus. And because no one wants to play Scrooge, Santa is above suspicion. No-one questions his comings and goings.

In the United States, fantasy is an industry. The personalities created by Disneyland, Hollywood, and the TV network are national celebrities and the image they create is often accepted as more real than the person behind it. And while the European Sinter Klaas and Father Christmas imbibe the occasional tipple and reveal a human weakness for indulging in the good things in life, the American Santa Claus is a professional goody-two-shoes who out-Disneys Disney, seemingly benevolent but perhaps a little sinister, waiting for his chance to move in and

trade on people's dreams.

In England Father Christmas is losing popularity. The London costumiers keep both Santa Claus and Father Christmas outfits. The former is the short belted red tunic with a fur trimmed nightcap, the latter a long red robe with a hood. The demand for Father Christmas grows less each year, and even bastions of department store tradition such as Harrods and Selfridges have gone over to Santa.

He has become totally international. In China they call him *Dun Che Lao Ren* (Christmas Old Man) or *Lang Khoeng* (Good Old Father). In Brazil he is known as *Papa Noel* and in Muslim Turkey, *Baba Noel*. In Australia, among the bikinied bathers on Bondi Beach, a surfboat manned by muscle-bound lifeguards runs up the shingle and out step a troupe of Santa Clauses. And even the ancient Arctic domain of the Nisser and Nikolai Chudovorits is now the destination of jet charters flying tourists to a Santa theme park in Lapland.

In Russia, Father Frost reigns supreme and has spread his travels into the countries of Eastern Europe as the true red by the bed. For, like the 17th-century Puritans, the 20th-century Bolsheviks banned Christmas as a holiday. So there is no way that Santa Claus, the symbol of capitalist decadence, will gain a foothold . . . or will he? Santa Claus has even arrived in Bethlehem where he works for the local toyshop, delivering purchases around the town on Christmas Eve. It is a long way from *Away In a Manger*.

Demoted and disregarded in his tomb in Bari, what would St Nicholas say about it all? In Protestant Europe he was turned into a pagan; in Russia he was purged; in the New World his early success in show-business has become a tool for commercial exploitation.

In 1951, in front of the Cathedral at Dijon in France, an effigy of Père Nöel was burned before several hundred Sunday School children and denounced by the clergy as *'a Saxon myth who never existed except in parents' annual lies to their children'*. He was vilified as a usurper and a heretic who was paganising Christmas. Thirty years later an Anglican vicar criticised Santa as an 'evil prowler' frightening children with the prospect of having their bedrooms invaded by a stranger:

Though he appears to be a great giver, he is actually a thief. For he is stealing the true value of Christmas. He directs our attention to selfish glitter, money, and a spirit that comes out of a bottle. His bottomless sack feeds our base emotions and he represents getting rather than giving.

Since then, the Dominican friars who look after his tomb in Bari have been busy researching his life and compiling evidence to have him reinstated. As far as they are concerned, the Vatican decision was based on a lack of information, and they hope to have the case reviewed.

There are other supporters too. Some years ago, two Chicago physicists calculated that to visit everybody in one night, Santa would have to travel at nearly 70,000 miles per second and would visit an estimated 2,000 million homes. This, they said, was no problem, assuming that he derives his enormous energy from a theoretical rotating 'black hole' at the North Pole!

Part cultural attaché, part million dollar mogul, the promoter of gifts is now very different from the character Professor Moore revealed to his children in 1822. In the best tradition of American success stories, he has risen from a humble immigrant into a multi-national mogul with a multi-billion dollar turnover. With success he has become depersonalised, a commercial clone available in a variety of models – white, black, or oriental; dwarf or giant; male or female – a Santa Claus person who water-skis, parachutes, flies, helicopters, and even does a striptease if the money is right.

In fact Santa's image has become so tarnished that even the Vatican came to the conclusion that he was probably an imposter. Saints were not formally canonised until the time of Pope Gregory (590–604). Before this, saints like Nicholas were simply acclaimed by local communities. When the Roman Catholic Church reformed its calendar in 1968 it was felt that St Nicholas's reputation was based more on legend than on historical fact, and so his feast day was discontinued.

Santa Claus is faced with an identity crisis. He is schizophrenic. Which of all his multiple personalities will triumph in the Christmases to come? Generation after generation families have introduced their children to the legends, and in one guise or another Santa has survived for over 1700 years. Now he has reached perhaps the biggest crisis of his career and, as in his past, so his future will be a reflection of the values of the society which we in our turn create for the generations to come.